Understanding the Agile Manifesto
A Brief & Bold Guide to Agile

Understanding the Agile Manifesto
A Brief & Bold Guide to Agile

Larry Apke

Lulu Publishing
2015

Copyright © 2015 by Larry Apke

All rights reserved. This book or any portion thereof may not be reproduced or used in any manner whatsoever without the express written permission of the publisher except for the use of brief quotations in a book review or scholarly journal.

First Printing: 2015

ISBN 978-1-312-86391-0

Published by Lulu Publishing

Contents

Introduction 5

The Agile Values 8

Individuals & Interactions 9

Working Software 14

Customer Collaboration 17

Responding to Change 21

The Agile Principles 23

Satisfy the Customer 24

Changing Requirements 27

Deliver Working Software 30

Work Together 33

Motivated Individuals 35

Conveying Information 38

The Primary Measure of Progress 41

Sustainable Development 46

Technical Excellence & Good Design 51

Simplicity is Essential 56

Self-Organizing Teams 59

Team Adjustments 63

About the Author 73

Introduction

Before jumping into the Agile Manifesto, it's important to understand not only why we should do Agile, but why Agile is successful.

The answer can be expressed in one word – feedback.

The waterfall methodology fails because it makes some fundamental assumptions that are completely incorrect. Waterfall assumes that software development is complicated. Waterfall can succeed, but mainly in solving problems that do not require feedback and adjustment.

Agile was created as a response to the failures of waterfall and understands that software development is mainly a complex undertaking involving people who must harness continual feedback to solve difficult problems.

Want proof? Look at the those things we generally associated with Agile – daily standups, pair programming, test driven design (TDD), behavior driven development (BDD), continuous integration, iteration reviews, retrospectives, card walls, code reviews, static code analysis and so on. What are these other than ways to gain continuous feedback? The Agile part comes in when we actually take this feedback and use it to make changes to our plans. Agile changes based on feedback. Waterfall rarely changes, but then again, with the paucity of feedback, how and why would it?

Waterfall was a mistake. It may be that it can work from time to time when applied to complicated problems, but it is sorely lacking when it comes to the complex problems software development faces. It could be that it continues to be used because there are infrequent successes that occasionally provide reinforcement, a complete lack of understanding of what software development is by people making decisions and our inherent human ability to avoid change. It took decades to convince doctors to wash their hands, so it will take some time to convince some people to adopt the Agile philosophy.

Nevertheless, the why of Agile is simple – in a complex world, frequent feedback and adapting to that feedback is not only highly effective, but necessary to long term survival.

The Agile Values

Individuals & Interactions

Some may say that software development values have gotten muddled because the majority of companies now value processes and tools more than individuals and interactions. Obviously in order to create better software this needs to be corrected!

Those of us challenged with transforming organizations to Agile can see the attraction of putting processes and tools over individuals and interactions. There are a great number of individuals in positions of power and influence who believe that if they can find the right processes and get people to slavishly follow then we can deliver.

In this mindset, people are resources; chess pieces to be moved around. The chance to be master of the universe is intoxicating and plays well into our mistaken notion that we can be in control. However, let me be clear that this is a fool's errand because it doesn't work well in the real world and it *especially* doesn't work well in software development.

In some respects, it reminds me of socialism in that if we only move the right levers and offer the right incentives then we can get complex social constructs to behave in predefined ways. And the ideas around process management can be traced back to the theory of a mechanistic world that can be known and tamed.

We would be better to look at theories of complex systems for inspiration. Some things look great on paper (for example, the Dallas Cowboys would always win if they didn't actually have to take the field), but what looks good in theory doesn't always work well in practice. The Soviet Union fell because grand plans do not necessarily work well with real human beings because humans are not machines, therefore they will not behave predictably. For instance, real humans do not like being micro-managed and the majority of workers are motivated more by intrinsic factors than extrinsic rewards.

Humans are messy. They are individuals. They work well with some people and not well with others. They cannot be treated as if they are all the same.

For instance, I have three children of different ages. Therefore, I treat the seven year-old much differently than the twenty one year-old. And though they share genetics and a similar environment, they each have a unique personality and how we interact and react to each other is vastly different. There is not one playbook that will necessarily work with each child, so why would we expect it to work with every individual at work? Of course, we all strive for fairness and there are certain ways we should all be treated, but one process fits all? I think not.

Teams are made up of individuals, every team has its own individual personality. Even if I found a process that works well with one team, it might not work with another. That is not to say that there aren't universal processes for teams, but the more prescriptive and detailed the less likely it is that it will work with everyone (Think waterfall). This is why Agile methodologies, like Scrum, rely on fewer controls. All teams should share the philosophy of Agile, but even basic methodologies (Scrum, Kanban and others) do not need to be shared by all since the overall needs of the team and the individuals comprising the teams are separate.

Just as one process will not work with all individuals or teams, one tool (or set of tools) cannot work for all teams. The Agile Manifesto doesn't say that tools are not important, but their use should be subservient to the individuals and should not interfere with the interactions among individuals.

Software development is communication and creativity; it only works when people are treated like individuals so their inherent creativity can be evidenced.

Furthermore, individuals on a team must constantly interact but processes and tools are often in the way of this collaboration. The writers of the Agile Manifesto knew that processes and tools were necessary to software development, but our very human need to have an illusion of control can lead us to value processes and tools over individuals and interactions.

Working Software

Of the four Agile values, this value is probably the least understood and often misinterpreted. It certainly does not say that there should be no documentation as some developers and teams propose. It does say that there is more value to actual software than comprehensive documentation.

And while I have a great deal of affection for the Agile Manifesto, the original writers could have been more specific to remove some of the confusion and misinformation that has sprung up around this value. It would've been more appropriate if the original writers had said, "Working software over comprehensive requirements and design documentation."

This level of specificity would keep teams from using the excuse that there should be no documentation at all. We have to remember that the writers of the Agile Manifesto wrote a reaction to what they perceived to be shortcomings in the prevalent way software was delivered. In that phase—gated approach, copious documentation of requirements and design were produced before any substantive software was developed. Prior to the Agile Manifesto, comprehensive documentation could be delivered but working software was either not delivered or poorly delivered because so much emphasis was placed on requirements and design documentation. In other words, documentation is important but it should be less important than actually building the software. What is the use of great documentation of a system that is poorly or not fully built? Also, documentation tends to be easily outdated so I suspect that the manifesto writers were also alluding to this fact.

Why create copious amounts of documentation that does not match the final product? Or why spend all our time updating copious documentation as the product changes?

There are usually two types of documentation — internal facing documentation, like design and requirements documents, and external facing documentation, like user manuals. So far my argument has been for internal facing documentation. Agile addresses internal facing documentation with user stories and acceptance criteria. I like to attack internal documentation using Behavior Driven Development (BDD) since then the code always matches the internal system documentation.

But what about external documentation? The Manifesto writers would argue that good design would preclude the need for end-user documentation. They would agree since they are user-focused and they would be more supportive this type of documentation versus internal documentation.

Customer Collaboration

We all have customers. If we didn't there would be no reason to do what we do. If we didn't there would be no one to pay our invoices. And when someone agrees to pay you for work, they generally want to have some kind of agreement on the nature of the work for the money that is being paid. This agreement is usually put in writing and *voila*, we have a contract.

This is an important part of the process and as everyone knows, contracts are valuable documents for both the customer and yourself. But as the Agile Manifesto states, it's important to not get caught up in negotiation fever. While it is a good thing to have an agreement before work begins, there are a number of unfortunate aspects to even having such an agreement.

The main problem is complexity. Software development, by its very nature, is a complex endeavor, dependent on communication and creativity to succeed. While it would be wonderful if all our customers were omniscient, they are often far from it. If we were building a house, we could easily choose things like materials and the architecture of the project and expect that the final building will resemble what was originally agreed upon. Such a thing is rarely true in something as complex as software development, but it hasn't stopped people from trying.

There is a field of study called complexity theory that applies well to software development.
In Joseph Pelrine's article, *On Understanding Software Agility — A Social Complexity Point Of View,* he writes:

"Many people still regard building software as a complicated undertaking, but in fact it is a defining example of a complex or a 'wicked' problem. The concept of wicked problems was originally proposed by Horst Rittel and Marcus

Webber. Wicked problems have incomplete, contradictory, and changing requirements; and solutions to them are often difficult to recognize as such, because of complex interdependencies. Rittel and Webber stated that while attempting to solve a wicked problem, the solution of one of its aspects may reveal or create other, even more complex problems. Rittel expounded on the nature of ill—defined design and planning problems, which he termed 'wicked' (that is, messy, circular, aggressive) to contrast against the relatively 'tame' problems of mathematics, chess, or puzzle solving."

If the nature of software development is indeed "wicked", then trying to agree on all the requirements at the outset in contractual form is not only wasteful but also counterproductive. A much better way is to form an understanding with broad-brush strokes and work together to attack the problems, hence the need for collaboration over contract negotiation. The same is true when the customer is internal. This is why Scrum has a product owner who is available daily for the team to work on the software. Instead of assuming we know everything at the beginning and then have mind—numbing change reviews and contract addenda, is it not better to forge a lasting partnership? I would rather have a long-term relationship full of trust, not one that is shallow.

Responding to Change

Of the four Agile values, this is the least controversial and most self-explanatory. Although this may seem obvious, it is still important to discuss and understand. It serves as a reminder as something that we should never forget, even if we think its common sense.

When contemplating this value, my mind always gravitates to Chevy Chase from *National Lampoon's Vacation*. Project managers are like Clark Griswolds, as in rushing headlong towards the world's largest ball of mud known as code.

The interesting thing about big, upfront design is the gall it takes to believe that all is known at the beginning of a complex endeavor. This hearkens back to some of my earlier writing where I argue that those in charge of software development decisions (e.g. team size, composition, physical location) have no clue about software development. And again, complexity theory tells us that complex problems are solved by feedback and that small changes can lead to large consequences. This argues less for upfront design and more for something called emergent design. This can only be accomplished when our development techniques allow for emergent design - hence my nearly fanatical support for BDD (Behavior Driven Development) and CD (Continuous Delivery).

The world is ever changing and complex. Software development relies heavily on creativity and communication. These things are only possible when we leave the safety of upfront design and embrace uncertainty along with the expected. As well, it is only possible when we respond to change and create a development environment, both tactical and cultural, where creativity and communication can occur.

The Agile Principles

Satisfy the Customer

As an Agile coach, I am in the Agile transformation business. Coaches are rarely employed when an organization understands the philosophy and properly implements an Agile framework or methodology. In my experience, those that are most challenged are those who seem to concentrate on the ceremonies while failing to focus on the big picture concerns – those more interested in "doing" rather than "being".

The first Agile principle is that our highest priority is to satisfy the customer through early and continuous delivery of valuable software. This provides the grounding teams need as they pursue the Agile path. One things I find interesting about the Agile principles is where the principles are vague and when they are specific or prescriptive.

In this case, "early and continuous" are vague, but "highest priority" is certainly not. While daily stand ups, planning, grooming and so on are important components, we should never forget to continually ask ourselves, are we satisfying our customers? Not because it is merely important, but because it is the *most* important.

The phrase "early and continuous" is important because we can provide users with functionality in a more just-in-time manner and allow for more frequent feedback. That is critically important when we are working on a complex endeavor, like creating software. This also tangentially points to some of the best software development practices, like continuous integration & delivery, Behavior Driven Development (BDD) and Test Driven Development (TDD).

The phrase "valuable software" reminds us to always be vigilant that we are actually concentrating our efforts on the most valuable stories, those that will give the most return on our investment. We should always keep in mind the Pareto principle – we receive 80 percent of our benefit from 20 percent of our stories. That means there is a huge value in the work not done!

As always, whenever I face a tough issue in Agile transformations, I regularly look back at the Agile Manifesto and its values and principles – especially the one that reminds me what the highest priority of software development actually is.

Changing Requirements

The world changes fast. The software development world changes faster. Locking into a long term plan and remaining steadfast to that plan might bring comfort when the world around us is awash in change, but it doesn't give the flexibility necessary to remain competitive.

If we can react to market changes faster than our competition, we can harness change for our competitive advantage. And we should not believe that market share or size can save us because Facebook barely existed only five years ago and I guarantee that the next Facebook is being made in a dorm room right now.

Typical waterfall projects are very plan driven and change is discouraged. They rely on things like a change review board to approve any changes to scope. In most places, I have seen people executing the projects would rather undergo a root canal than to present changes to the review board! On the other hand, Agile requires a more value-driven approach. Agile strives to make sure that value is relevant and can adjust with changes like environmental and competitive pressure, emerging opportunities and unseen potentiality. Nevertheless, never confuse welcoming changing requirements with chaos.

Using Agile or scrum is not an excuse to be unorganized or lack vision. Chasing one BSO (Bright Shiny Object) after another is the surest way to create a disorganized mess of software which leads to a competitive disadvantage and a demoralized workforce.

I once worked with a company that allowed its product owner to change nearly all (about 90 percent) of a team's stories the Friday before sprint planning. This led to the team not having the time to groom their stories effectively and resulted in very long sprint planning sessions with estimates of work that were wildly inaccurate. In the end, the quality of the software suffered, the team's productivity was reduced, the team was rarely able to implement what the business desired and there was a growing animosity between development and business. It was a downward cycle that the company still suffers from today.

If chaos like the above can be avoided then Agile's second principle proves to be extremely powerful in helping us continually concentrate on emerging value and giving our customers the competitive advantage that they all seek.

Deliver Working Software

While there are many people who believe that the key reason to adopt Agile frameworks and methods is for increased productivity, I tend to find this to be more a healthy byproduct of a team working together over time (and thus could be found in other methodologies).

The real benefits of Agile lies in greater transparency, predictability and faster time to market. The third Agile principle speaks directly to these, especially quicker time to market.

When organizations I have coached are having issues with Agile adoption, I have come to expect that they will have difficulty upholding this principle because it requires the most organizational change. It is no coincidence that there is a greater desire for "dev-ops" as Agile transformation is attempted by more, especially large organizations.

In one of my regular presentations, I argue that there are two things necessary for Agile success over the long term: One of these is Continuous Delivery (CD), or at least continuous integration (CI). The other necessity is acceptance test driven development (ATDD), with my preference being behavior driven development (BDD).

It is difficult to deliver working software often, but it is critical. In fact, even if a team is not good at delivering working software often, there is a tremendous amount of value to be obtained trying to deliver software often if only to find out the reasons why your team cannot.

In consulting with organizations I am often asked to merely optimize Agile teams, but the real work of transforming to a complete Agile system is not considered. These hybrid waterfall-Agile organizations are nothing more than waterfall process with Agile development and in a lot of cases even this Agile development itself is not very agile.

I often ask organizations a simple question, "How long does it take you to deliver even a single line of code change into production?"

This is one simple question to gauge your agility. If the answer is more than a day or so, then there is a lot of work that needs to be done for continuous integration or continuous delivery.

I find it amusing to think that a "big bang" approach with months of code changes can be successfully delivered if it is so difficult to deliver only those few changes that are a result of a single iteration.

Work Together

I constantly quote this principle verbatim to all the teams I coach because it is the only completely prescriptive principle. While other principles use more vague words like "early", "late" or "shorter", "daily" is not open to negotiation or interpretation. The word "must" is also unequivocal as are the roles described.

That prompts the following question – why were the founders of Agile so strident with this principle while allowing for broader interpretation with all other values and principles?

To me the answer is simple – in order to avoid even the smallest chance of misinterpretation it is crucial for everyone to understand how critical daily communication is between business and development. It also gives us a clue as to what the most important aspect found lacking in failing projects is.

In other words, unless you have business needs properly communicated to development through daily interaction, chances are good that your project will fail. This simple reality – the inability for business and development to communicate – underlines all of the failed projects I have witnessed in my many years of experience.

Interestingly, this principle also is a good measure of a company's ability to successfully transform to Agile successfully. A great number of companies that experience Agile failure do so as a direct result of their inability to live the Agile principles, especially in relation to the fourth Agile principle. If you want your team or organization to be Agile, but you have not ensured an environment where business and development can work together daily, your chances of actual success is slim to none, so please do not claim that Agile has failed you when, in reality, you have failed Agile.

Motivated Individuals

If I had to take exception to any value or principle, this would have to be the one. While I have the utmost of respect for the original Agile signatories, they made a slight mistake because this principle refers to *only* projects. I have ranted often enough about the distinction between project and product management, but it is important to understand that Agile works best when we build a product (not a project) mindset.

By having a principle that mentions projects, this might hinder folks from transforming their project-centric thinking to product-centric thinking. That slight semantic problem aside, this principle highlights the need for motivated individuals in order to complete quality work.

Prior to Agile, people were assigned to death-march projects, treated like widgets as to their work and children as to their maturity, needing to be supervised at every step of the way lest they make a mistake.

This is called Taylorism and has been proven to work well with rote and manual tasks, but has been scientifically shown to not work with knowledge work and workers. I have written previously about this in reference to the book *Drive*, which has wonderful information about motivation and the science behind it.

Another aspect of this principle is trust. The very fact that we do not trust our people leads to a whole host of detrimental behavior and waste, whether it manifests as command and control management, approval bottlenecks, ridiculous amounts of upfront requirements and so on. I highly encourage people to read Patrick Leoncini's *Five Dysfunctions of a Team,* where he explains that other dysfunctions cannot be overcome until we overcome the primary issue of trust.

This principle also refers to environment and support. In my coaching engagements and throughout my career, I am constantly amazed by the sheer number of managers who fail to realize that their primary role is to support those folks assigned to their care. Managers must be true servant leaders (and the scrum framework calls this out in the position of scrum master as servant leader) for their people. The front line workers are not there to serve their managers. It is up to management to create an environment that allows workers to do their work.

Conveying Information

Since there are so many misconceptions about miscommunication around Agile, I created my business cards to contain the entire Agile Manifesto so that when people confuse scrum framework with Agile philosophy or say, "This is Agile!" I can hand them my card and say, "No, this is Agile."

Then I let them know that Agile is nothing more than a philosophy, a series of values and principles.

In my mind, a principle is something that could be debated. When it comes to methods of communication, it would be very difficult to debate that something other than face-to-face conversation is best so this reads more like a fact than a principle.

A quick Google search on the topic produces a lot of results in confirmation that face-to-face communication is the "gold standard of communication" and an impressive body of research demonstrates that face-to-face is the most information-rich medium.

The question is, why this would need to be called out in the Agile principles? I think the reason is that all too often software development companies forget this important fact.

I point out in my presentation about complexity and Cynefin that most software development is complex. As such it requires a great deal of communication and collaboration. It is not something that we can just gather requirements and parse these out to large and disparate teams across the globe (unless, of course, your project is truly complicated and not complex).

Working in an Agile way requires that we come to a good understanding of what is desired through frequent, high-quality communication. The fourth principle addresses the frequency while this principle attends to the richness and quality of the conversation. I always tell my teams that they need to make sure to keep some whitespace free on their whiteboards since the most effective communication is face-to face at a whiteboard so that ideas can be discussed in all the richness of our senses and where examples can be used to quickly iterate through ideas.

In the end, all the Agile principles and values must be viewed through the lens of being a reaction to the mistakes that were perpetrated before. It is readily apparent that this principle was added to the other eleven to be a constant reminder that documentation only allows us to avoid failure, but real face-to-face conversations lead to a much deeper understanding that will (hopefully) lead us to success.

The Primary Measure of Progress

Metrics. Metrics. Metrics. We love numbers. We measure and put numbers to all kinds of things. We use these numbers to mark our projects as green, yellow and red (of course, the project is always green until there are a few weeks left when someone finally blinks and acknowledges reality and begins to use yellow or, god forbid, red).

Unfortunately, in our headlong rush to create metrics we tend to forget the why of what we are doing. Numbers and statuses become an end unto themselves.

There are a myriad of problems with this. First, what get measured gets done. In our rush to get numbers we need to be very careful because measuring the wrong things will lead to all kinds of behaviors that can be detrimental to long term sustainability. For example, one company I worked for misunderstood the team velocity metric and rewarded teams based on the number of points completed. What happened? Over time the point values for stories increased so that teams would look better but the amount of throughput did not increase. This misuse of story points completely invalidated their even relative gross sizes to a point where they could no longer be used to give accurate information back to the business of what teams were capable over the long term. In other words, the valuable ability to be predictable was lost to service a poorly misunderstood metric.

The next problem is that we tend to measure those things that are easy to measure not necessarily those things that are important. There is an old joke about a drunk man looking for his keys under the street lamp:

"A policeman sees a drunk man searching for something under a streetlight and asks what the drunk has lost. He says he lost his keys and they both look under the streetlight together. After a few minutes the policeman asks if he is sure he lost them here, and the drunk replies, no, he lost them in the park. The policeman asks why he is searching here, and the drunk replies, 'This is where the light is."

If we only measure only those things that are easy to measure, as opposed to those things that really matter, then we are no better than that drunk man looking under the streetlight because the light is better. As he will never find his keys, we may never find the truth by measuring what is easy versus what is important.

I often quote from Deming when discussing measurements. He states, "The most important things cannot be measured," and, "The most important things are unknown or unknowable."

There is a very simple example that I often use when explaining this concept.

I ask people if they have children. Do they love them? How do you go about measuring this love? Do you use minutes spent? Money spent? A combined weighted score that takes into account both money and time? Or do you do some regular poll of your children to see how much loved they feel on a Likert scale?

Obviously, the love a parent has for his or her children is of paramount importance, but this is something very hard to measure.

I once spoke to a group of project managers and explained that we measure way too much. We measure things that are either easy to measure or do not really result in better behavior. You would have thought that I advocated clubbing baby seals! They decided that I was against all measurement. The answer is not that I am against all measures, but that I know that measures are limited in value due to the reasons outlines above (and many other human biases), so we need to measure less and be very careful what we measure.

In software development, the primary measure of progress has to be working software that meets the needs of the end users. Of course we can measure other things, but there is no more important measure and all other measures need to be subservient to our ability to produce working software.

Sustainable Development

When I think on this principle I cannot help but think about the potential "dark side" of Agile and how it can be misunderstood and implemented incorrectly. It also reminds me of an interesting story I was told by one of my coaching colleagues recently.

Once upon a time a company hired a very talented vice president of software development. Unfortunately, when this brave soul entered employment, the amount of technical debt in the code was enormous. This was a situation that needed to be fixed because this pasta code was very expensive to maintain and made it difficult to deliver software quickly and with quality.

The company's leadership heard about Agile and decided that this was the answer to all their problems so they set about sprinting. Since the concepts are so easy, they felt they could forge ahead without expert Agile help. In their quest for agility, they found that they could indeed write code faster, but without proper guidance they forgot about the concept of sustainability and did nothing more than create technical debt faster. Unfortunately for our VP, the pleas to adopt sustainable agility went unheeded and six months was all the VP could take before moving on.

The bottom line is that many companies misuse Agile because they think by being Agile they can cheat the iron triangle of development. What too few people realize is that you don't choose two of three sides of the iron triangle because it's actually an iron square. You choose three of four sides (scope, resources, schedule and quality - as Jeff Atwood refers to it, an Iron Stool). You misuse Agile when you choose everything but quality because the code becomes unsustainable over time and agility becomes mired in the big ball of mud you have created.

The misguided desire to emphasize speed over quality leads to the accumulation of technical debt and is a symptom of project-centric thinking, not product-centric. Overtime, you will no longer get speed or quality, and your ability to sustain Agile over long periods of time is compromised.

I try to run at least a few miles every day, but I do not sprint the entire run. If I did, I would barely make it more than about a quarter of a mile. This is why I have begun to prefer the term iteration over sprint. Sprinting goes against this principle because sprinting is, almost by definition, unsustainable. It certainly is not "constant pace indefinitely".

I argue that in order to maintain constant pace indefinitely there are two things a team must do and an organization must support - Acceptance Test Driven Development (ATDD) and Continuous Integration / Delivery (CI/CD).

I believe that BDD (Behavior Driven Development) is the best means of accessing ATDD (and TDD) so I have taught that to my clients with spectacular success.

Without ATDD and CI/CD, all teams are doing is what I call feature chasing. The question is not one of sustainability, but how many and how quickly can I deliver new features. While this might be important for startups, most are not involved in such high competition that chasing features at the expense of quality and long term sustainability is ludicrous. Even those who must feature chase to remain competitive must recognize that they are creating technical debt that must be paid, and paid quickly, before servicing the "interest" on the debt is all that can be afforded.

Interestingly enough, though many people believe that employing ATDD, TDD and CI/CD slows the progress of software delivery, my experience is that, with very little training and a healthy dose of discipline, the gains far outweigh the investment. This is obvious if we look at the product and not just the project, but my experience shows that even within the misguided and arbitrary project, the payoff is realized.

I have a number of teams that I have coached that delivered high quality software into production in short project time frames precisely because, and not in spite of, BDD. As Bob Martin states, "The only way to go fast is to go well," and no one is more recognized as an expert on quality code than him.

My last point is related to the above in that one of the greatest dangers of feature chasing is not just that we tend to accumulate technical debt faster, but it generally pressures us to not take advantage of training opportunities like learning TDD, BDD and the like. With technology changing so quickly it is critical that our people make certain to invest their time not just chasing features, but building the skills necessary for sustainable development so they can maintain a constant pace indefinitely.

Technical Excellence & Good Design

This principle is much like the one previous about sustainable development. Agile doesn't ask us to shortcut quality and increase technical debt in an effort to deliver software faster. It is precisely because we do not shortcut quality and incur technical debt that we are able to move faster.

I have worked with many teams to introduce Behavior Driven Development (BDD) because, among a great number of other advantages, BDD allows developers an easier way to access the practice of Test Driven Development (TDD). And, in my experience, TDD is the only way I have seen out of the practice of "Big Up Front Design".

Big Up Front Design is generally a waterfall practice in that architects and designers spend a great amount of time before coding begins to attempt to foresee all possible design considerations in advance so that the final design could be implemented without issues. The problems with this approach are outlined wonderfully in Martin Fowler's "Is Design Dead?" blog.

The one I would concentrate most on is the issue of changing requirements. Since most of software development falls in the complex quadrant, it generally has a great deal of nonlinearity. This means that any small change in requirements can have a great ripple effect, usually nullifying the extensive work that designers and architects have created.

If you want a rule of thumb measure of an organization's (or team's) relative agility, bring up the word "refactor". A rigid organization will recoil in horror while an Agile one will recognize refactoring as desirable.

The answer to nonlinearity is the concept of evolutionary design and this is simply not possible without refactoring and refactoring is simply not possible without a safety net. That safety net is created by a suite of tests that were created as a result of TDD (using something like BDD) and are leveraged via Continuous Integration and Continuous Delivery.

With respect to this principle, continuous attention to technical excellence is expressed through the XP practices of BDD/TDD and CI/CD, learning how to create testable requirements (via BDD), which are expressed through tests created prior to coding (TDD), and through near instantaneous feedback (CI/CD).

I can be assured that my refactoring of design addresses not only the new requirements, but also the legion of existing requirements (through automated regression), so that nonlinearity is not expressed through regression defects in the final product. Because of the technical excellence above, I can then use evolutionary design to create not just "good" but excellent design.

"This might all sound fine," you say, "but I live in the real world and it doesn't work for us because of (fill in your favorite excuse)."

To you I say, yes, *it does work.*

No matter what your situation, you can leverage the above practices. That is not to say that it won't be challenging, because you may be struggling with existing technical debt, but it is possible if your organization had the understanding of the costs of not adhering to this principle. For the skeptics out there I leave you with a little story:

There was one team that I worked with to teach BDD/TDD and pushed them to adopt these practices. Though they were initially skeptical, they did it anyway. After only a few short days, they began to see the method to my madness and roundly declared that this was the way that all software should be developed. After a few months of success, they were asked to present what they learned to other teams. Like a proud father I stood in the background and listened to what they said. Not only did they say that they couldn't imagine doing software development without these practices, but that there were times that they felt pressured to produce software faster that led to shortcutting the processes. Every time they did, it was this code that was identified later to have defects that they had to spend time fixing.

Because the time spent finding and fixing code that wasn't created using TDD was greater than if they had slowed down and done the initial coding properly, trying to write code faster by neglecting technical excellence was actually slower in the long run. To this day these folks that I had the pleasure of teaching a bit of technical excellence to email me from time to time to tell me that they have convinced yet another team (or vendor) to pursue technical excellence. Why? Because continuous attention to technical excellence and good design enhances agility.

Simplicity is Essential

In 2002, Jim Johnson of the Standish Group (known for their reports on software project success), presented findings of features and functions used in a typical system. The number of features that were never or rarely used totaled a whopping 64 percent, while sometimes, often and always weighed in with 16 percent, 13 percent and 7 percent respectively. For those acquainted with the Pareto principle (80/20 Rule), notice how the often and always used features – those things we should concentrate on building for our customers and those things that bring us the most value – is exactly 80 percent.

In other words, a great deal of our effort is generally spent creating things that customers do *not* use or want.

A lot of times this is a forgotten principle as people get caught up in the world of implementing stories and forget that there may be a plethora of stories that don't need to ever be implemented.

What value is there is doing work faster and better if we are doing four times the amount of work that we need to do?

This principle fits well with the concept of business and development working daily. Business needs to be intensely involved with the process, if for nothing more than identifying the 80 percent of the work that we really don't have to do.

Just think of the amount of money that could be saved every year by reducing project scope to only those features and functions that are actually used! Think of how quickly we could deliver functionality! Think of how many more "projects" we could complete!

While simplicity provides huge benefits with regards to the stories and work that we choose to implement, it also applies to the implementation of stories that we choose. As I have written about so many times, by using techniques like BDD and TDD, we write only the software that is necessary to implement the acceptance criteria and are not tempted to "gold plate".

TDD provides us with a certain simplicity at the code level while also providing us the ability to allow our code to evolve over time to satisfy changing requirements. Simplicity of code allows us to refactor code mercilessly which is essential to agility over the long term.

In the end, simplicity of what we do and how we do it results in producing the most valuable software in a high quality manner and this is essential to being Agile.

Self-Organizing Teams

I have often argued that the founders of Agile did not provide reasons why their approaches worked, just that they did. There was empirical evidence, proven by doing the work, or, as they state in the beginning of the Manifesto – uncovering better ways of developing software by doing it and helping others do it. From their pragmatic approach, they figured out that better software was created by following the values and principles. One of those discoveries was that better software was created by self-organizing teams.

One of the things I speak of during my talk on Complexity Theory and Cynefin (Complexity Theory and Why Waterfall Development Works (Sometimes)), is that most software development is complex and that is the reason that Agile works well and is generally preferable to waterfall. Those projects that might benefit from waterfall are those that are complicated, those where all the answers can be known up front and experts are effective. Agile works better when projects are complex, those where all the answers cannot be known upfront and big upfront expert analysis is a liability. Also, according to George Rzevski, one of the seven criteria for complexity is self-organization, in which complex systems are capable of self-organization in response to disruptive events. While this addresses the fact that a complex system will self-organize and does not address self-organizing teams in particular, I believe it does inform us that in response to complex systems the best use of people is to allow them to self-organize around the work.

In addition to the relationship with complexity theory, this principle also relates to the fact that it's the people who do the work that are the best to make decisions with regards to architectures, requirements and designs. While to most people this would be common sense, in the world of corporate IT, with its fetish for top-down command and control hierarchy, I have found this to be the exception.

In some cases I have found organizations so tied to the misunderstanding that software development is complicated (as opposed to complex), that work can be identified, analyzed and designed at one level and simply passed down to a lower level (usually to offshore), that they really have no conception of what Agile means when it talks about a team.

Even if they can be convinced that they need to think of teams as the people who actually do the work, it is usually too radical to expect people to actually know their jobs and be able to organize their own work. These organizations are stuck in the world of Taylor, but all the evidence shows us that knowledge workers are squarely in the world of Deming.

Pink, in his wonderful book *Drive: The Surprising Truth About What Motivates Us*, tells us that people are motivated by autonomy, mastery and purpose. Not surprisingly, self-organizing teams provide a healthy dose of all of these while receiving piecemeal work from "experts" is not at all motivating. No wonder that the best architectures, requirements, and designs emerge from self-organizing teams!

Team Adjustments

I coach the majority of my teams by first modeling the behavior that I expect. This allows teams to copy that behavior as I observe and correct so that it matches the modeled behavior. To achieve this a great deal of my time is spent as an active scrum master – and I love it! I love having the opportunity to interact with individuals on teams, but there are times, after literally hundreds of iteration plannings and reviews, thousands of daily stand ups, where it becomes difficult to keep things fresh. But this is never a problem when it comes to retrospectives, which is the topic of this last principle.

Retrospectives are my favorite of all the scrum activities because they represent the opportunity to reflect on how we are implementing and to adjust our behavior to be more effective.

I have said to my teams on many occasions that if I were forced to choose only one scrum ceremony, then I would choose, without hesitation or reservation, the retrospective. How can we ever expect to improve without it? What essential difference would an Agile project have over the many death march projects that teams have come to accept?

There are always better ways of doing business. As a team, we must frequently come together to honestly discuss current processes, evaluate potential alternatives and then experiment with alternatives to prove or disprove their value. Since not everything works well for every team, it is important that potential improvements are seen as experiments. It may be that it is the right thing to do, but it is merely not the right time.

I regularly tell my teams that we need to be scientists, as in we will try things that we do not know the result, because it is important to propose a theory and conduct a proper experiment.

I extend this concept of theory, implementation, observation and retrospective to more aspects of a team than just the official retrospective. For example, instead of time estimates, I propose that we have a theory on how long something will take and that we will test this theory by the end of the iteration. This provides a less threatening way of estimating so we can use real information to adjust our estimates to provide better estimates in the future. Regardless of the methodology, people will expect to understand what teams are capable of in the long term.

One thing I have noticed in regards to retrospectives is that teams struggling with Agile transformation will often drop the retrospective ceremony while keeping all the others. There are a number of possible reasons for this.

One reason is that the organization is so addicted to a top-down problem solving approach that management does not value identification and solving of problems at the team level so the meeting is quickly dropped. In these organizations honesty is rarely valued. Without honesty a proper retrospective cannot occur. One team I coached referred to their organization's "more than healthy aversion to reality".

I have also run into organizations that have a misguided desire to track team experiments. These "best practices" shops think that if we only identify what works for one team then we can codify this practice and force all others to adopt it. This is a big misunderstanding of Agile! While there may be "best practices" that work for all teams, this approach flies in the face of self-organization and ignores the fact that each team will mature at different times, so the practice that works for one team may be completely inappropriate for another. I certainly do not have the same expectations for my youngest child as my oldest.

Tracking experiments at the organization level also makes it more difficult to experiment, producing a chilling effect on teams. Instead of trusting that the team will attempt experiments that are best for their circumstance, there is one more hoop to jump, one more monitoring, one more instance of distrust and more business as usual.

As a result, teams experiment less, progress stagnates, the team experiences disincentives and any real change is exchanged for acceptable window dressing. After experiencing a few retrospectives under these constraints, it's not difficult to see why teams choose not to pursue more retrospectives.

There are times when teams have just not had coaching or training on how to properly conduct retrospectives. Some retrospectives become little more than glorified bitching sessions with no substantive changes discussed or attempted. This happens frequently when organizations tell teams that they will be Agile but do provide real support in removing the systemic obstacles to team success.

For every problem identified in a retrospective, there should be a corresponding action – even if that action is the need to escalate this item to management. Once something has been escalated to management, it is important for management to be held accountable to the team and, from time to time, report to the team on the progress of removing the impediments.

More importantly, since many problems may be systemic and beyond the ability of the team to change, it is incumbent on the scrum master to keep the team focused on the problems that can be solved. It is best to start small, for example with things like meeting times or rooms. Fixing small things that are in the team's power can go a long way in helping them to "gel" as a self-organizing team.

As to the retrospective meeting itself, there are quite a number of folks who have interesting facilitation techniques. Personally, I find most of these "team building" techniques forced, gimmicky and condescending to adults. If they work for you, fine, but they are not my way.

Here's how a typical retrospective meeting goes for me, I encourage everyone to try out my process to see if it works for your team. If it doesn't, then try, try again!

I keep my retrospectives simple and generic in asking:

- What went well?
- What could be improved?
- What actions can we take?

Gimmicks trade style for substance and if I do a good job of the "vanilla" retrospective, I find that I can keep it interesting and people engaged without tricks. The content of the discussion wins the day!

And I start each meeting with a simple statement of our intent, usually including something like Norm Kerth's Prime Directive, assuring the team that the purpose of our discussion is to improve our work as a team and nothing is personal.

The second thing that is often forgotten and critical to retrospective success, is to take some time at the beginning to review what was discussed and actions undertaken in the last retrospective. This way we can hold people accountable for delivering on the changes promised and not constantly tread over the same issues again and again.

Of course, if the same problems persist and it is a good jump off for discussion, there is no rule to say that we cannot re-discuss or re-emphasize something from a previous meeting.

Without this follow-up step I have witnessed a great number of teams with great intentions, but poor execution.

The next thing that we do is to go over the three columns:

- For each thing that we identify as going well (or not so well) the team is encouraged to come up with some kind of action that will help us continue the good and improve on the not so good.
- For every action that is taken, someone or a group is assigned to be accountable. If need be, a retrospective action can be planned during iteration planning to make sure there is time to get the work done.
- The meeting ends with a statement of appreciation for the team's honesty and courage in improving their work.

As far as timing of the meeting, I generally make sure that the retrospective is held in advance of the iteration planning so, as I mention above, any stories or tasks necessary for completion of retrospective actions can be accommodated.

Just as we try our best to eliminate work-in-progress for stories, we do the same with retrospective actions. Trying to do too many things at once is a recipe for disaster. Small incremental progress is the key!

While it is the last principle, as you can tell by the amount of commentary I have written around it, it is certainly not the least. In fact, I contend that a team cannot achieve sustainable agility without the frequent feedback and course correction that team reflection provides.

About the Author

Larry Apke is a Certified Scrum Master, Certified Scrum Professional and veteran Agile coach. He has worked in the financial, software, education healthcare and aviation industries as a results-oriented leader with proven success in devising and implementing solutions using Agile techniques. He has written for The Agile Record, Scrum Alliance and SD Times while also presenting to groups such as the Scrum Users Group, Java Users Group, Desert Code Camp and others.

Check out more of Larry's thoughts on Agile: www.agile-doctor.com

You can find him on LinkedIn, Twitter (@Agile_Doctor), Slideshare and Google Plus.

Printed in Great Britain
by Amazon